Nibble Nibble

POEMS FOR CHILDREN BY
Margaret Wise Brown

ILLUSTRATED BY LEONARD WEISGARD

HarperCollins*Publishers*

But ask now the beasts, and they shall teach thee;
and the fowls of the air and they shall tell thee:
Or speak to the earth, and it shall teach thee;
and the fishes of the sea shall declare unto thee.

Job 12:7, 8

A Young Scott Book
First published by Addison-Wesley Publishing Company
Nibble Nibble
Text copyright © 1959 by William R. Scott, Inc.
Illustrations copyright © 1959 by Leonard Weisgard

Library of Congress Cataloging in Publication Data
Brown, Margaret Wise, 1910–1952.
    Nibble nibble: poems for children.

(Young Scott books)
    Summary: Twenty-five poems, about insects, fish,
animals, birds, and the seasons.
    1. Nature—Juvenile poetry.   2. Children's poetry,
American.   [1. Nature—Poetry.   2. American poetry]
I. Weisgard, Leonard, 1916–   ill.   II. Title.
III. Series.
PS3503.R82184N5 1985   811'.52   84-43128
ISBN 0-201-09291-3

Printed in Mexico.

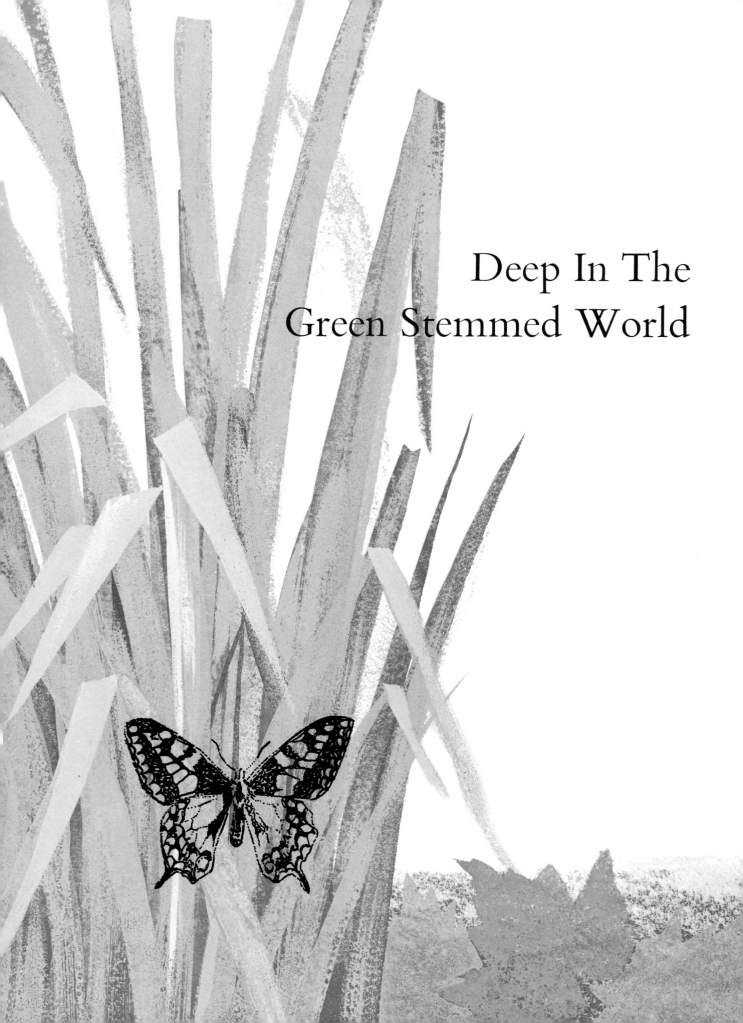

Deep In The Green Stemmed World

Song Of The Bugs

Some bugs pinch
And some bugs creep
Some bugs buzz themselves to sleep
Buzz Buzz Buzz Buzz
This is the song of the bugs.

Some bugs fly
When the moon is high
Some bugs make a light in the sky
Flicker, flicker firefly
This is the song of the bugs.

Green Stems

Little things that crawl and creep
In the green grass forests,
Deep in their long stemmed world
Where ferns uncurl
To a greener world
Beneath the leaves above them;
And every flower upon its stem
Blows above them there
The bottom of a geranium,
The back side of a trillium,
The belly of a bumble bee
Is all they see, these little things
Down so low
Where no bird sings
Where no winds blow,
Deep in their long stemmed world.

A Bug's Eye

Half way up the grass blade
Climbing high
A bug can see with his shining eye
A bug's enormous wide green sky
Above the grass blades
High High High.

On top of the grass blade
Grass blade high
A bug can see other bugs that fly
Into the wide enormous sky
That looked green below
To a bug's eye.

A Child's Delight

At the edge of the grass
Sat a bug in a glass
Wild
Caught by a child.
Too little to hug
Too precious to die
A firefly
Waiting for night
To flash his light
His wild green light
For a child's delight.

Bumble Bee

Black and yellow
Little fur bee
Buzzing away
In the timothy
Drowsy
Browsy
Lump of a bee
Rumbly
Tumbly
Bumbly bee.
Where are you taking
Your golden plunder
Humming along
Like baby thunder?
Over the clover
And over the hay
Then over the apple trees
Zoom away.

In The Darkness
Of The Sea

Four Fishing Boats

Four little boats
Late in the day
Hoisted their sails
And sailed away,
Over the ocean
And out toward the sky
Four little boats went sailing by.

They sailed all night
In the dark night light
Over high black waves
Of tremendous height,
They sailed all night.

Four little boats
Early next day
Furled their sails
In a quiet bay,
Then they waited for fish
To run that way
And the four little boats fished all day.

Fish Song

Oh the lobster and the fish
And the fish and the whale,
You can't catch a fish
With an old tin pail
And you can't catch a lobster
With a hook and a line
And you can't catch a whale at all.

Catch a lobster in a pot
And a fish on a line
Fish in the nets
When the weather is fine
But if you ever try to catch a whale,
He will knock you down flat
With a flip of his tail.

Sleepy Fish

Down in the sea where the fishes sleep
The water is wet
And the water is deep
And all the little fishes keep
Their eyes wide open while they sleep.

Song Of The Silver Fish

Little fishes in the sea
Swish your silver tails to lee,
Mind the blubber whale and shark,
Never swim far after dark.
In the darkness of the sea,
All the sunlight you can see
Is the waving pale green light
From a sun that's out of sight.
Moonfish, sunfish, starfish, ray
Take no sunlight from the day,
Sun and moon are far away.

The Fish With The Deep Sea Smile

They fished and they fished
Way down in the sea,
Down in the sea a mile,
They fished among all the fish in the sea
For the fish with the deep sea smile.

One fish came up from the deep of the sea,
From down in the sea a mile,
It had blue green eyes
And whiskers three
But never a deep sea smile.

One fish came up from the deep of the sea,
From down in the sea a mile,
With electric lights up and down his tail
But never a deep sea smile.

They fished and they fished
Way down in the sea,
Down in the sea a mile,
They fished among all the fish in the sea
For the fish with the deep sea smile.

One fish came up with terrible teeth,
One fish with long strong jaws,
One fish came up with long stalked eyes,
One fish with terrible claws.

They fished all through the ocean deep
For many and many a mile,
And they caught a fish with a laughing eye
But none with a deep sea smile.

And then one day they got a pull
From down in the sea a mile,
And when they pulled the fish into the boat
He smiled a deep sea smile.

And as he smiled, the hook got free
And then, what a deep sea smile!
He flipped his tail and swam away
Down in the sea a mile.

Ask Now The Animals

The Secret Song

Who saw the petals
   drop from the rose?
I, said the spider,
But nobody knows.

Who saw the sunset
   flash on a bird?
I, said the fish,
But nobody heard.

Who saw the fog
   come over the sea?
I, said the sea pigeon,
Only me.

Who saw the first
   green light of the sun?
I, said the night owl,
The only one.

Who saw the moss
   creep over the stone?
I, said the grey fox,
All alone.

Song Of The Bunnies

Bunnies zip
And bunnies zoom
Bunnies sometimes sleep till noon
Zoom Zoom Zoom Zoom
All through the afternoon
Zoom Zoom Zoom
This is the song of the bunnies.

Bunnies jump
And bunnies run
Bunnies also sit in the sun
This is the song of the bunnies.

The Bear And The Butterfly

The bear and the butterfly had a fight
All of the day and most of the night,
Till at last the bear lay waving his paws
And the butterfly lit on one of his jaws.
Oh, never struggle and never fight
With a butterfly on a moonlight night!

Little Donkey Close Your Eyes

Little Donkey on the hill
Standing there so very still
Making faces at the skies
Little Donkey close your eyes.

Little Monkey in the tree
Swinging there so merrily
Throwing cocoanuts at the skies
Little Monkey close your eyes.

Silly Sheep that slowly crop
Night has come and you must stop
Chewing grass beneath the skies
Silly Sheep now close your eyes.

Little Pig that squeals about
Make no noises with your snout
No more squealing to the skies
Little Pig now close your eyes.

Wild young birds that sweetly sing
Curve your heads beneath your wing
Dark night covers all the skies
Wild young birds now close your eyes.

Old black cat down in the barn
Keeping five small kittens warm
Let the wind blow in the skies
Dear old black cat close your eyes.

Little child all tucked in bed
Looking such a sleepy head
Stars are quiet in the skies
Little child now close your eyes.

The Rabbit Skip

Hop   Skip   Jump
A rabbit won't fight.

Hop   Skip   Jump
A rabbit won't bite.

Hop   Skip   Jump
A rabbit runs light.

Hop   Skip   Jump
He's out of sight.

Nibble Nibble Nibble

Nibble Nibble Nibble
Goes the mouse in my heart
Nibble Nibble Nibble
Goes the mouse in my heart
Nibble Nibble Nibble
Goes the mouse in my heart
And the mouse in my heart is
You.

Lippity Lippity Clip
Goes the rabbit in my heart
Lippity Lippity Clip
Goes the rabbit in my heart
Lippity Lippity Clip
Goes the rabbit in my heart
And the rabbit in my heart is
You.

Flippity Flippity Flop
Goes the fish in my heart
Flippity Flippity Flop
Goes the fish in my heart
Flippity Flippity Flop
Goes the fish in my heart
And the fish in my heart is
You.

Biff Bang Bang
Goes the hammer in my heart
Biff Bang Bang
Goes the hammer in my heart
Biff Bang Bang
Goes the hammer in my heart
And the hammer in my heart is
You.

Drum Drum Drum
Goes the drum in my heart
Drum Drum Drum
Goes the drum in my heart
Drum Drum Drum
Goes the drum in my heart
And the drum in my heart is
You.

Softly now beats the beat of my heart
Softly now beats the beat of my heart
Softly now beats the beat of my heart
All for the love of you.

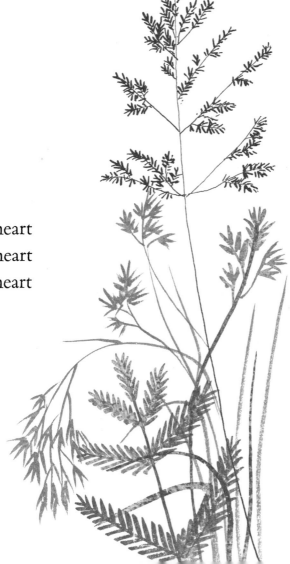

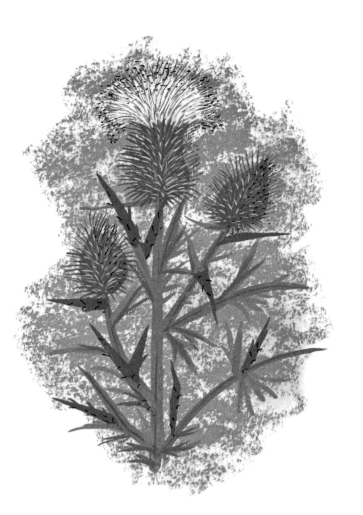

One By One

The Sad Sliced Onion

Once there was an onion.
The cook sliced it
And the cook began to cry
Boo! Hoo! Hoo!

The mother came to comfort the cook
And as she leaned over the sliced onion
The tears splashed from her eyes
Drip! Drip! Drip!

Then the father arrived
To comfort the mother
And he began to cry
Mrump! Mrump! Mrump!

The little boy came to comfort the father
And when he came near the onion
Tears rolled down his cheeks
Wah! Wah! Wah!

And they all cried
Boo! Hoo! Hoo!
Drip! Drip! Drip!
Mrump! Mrump!
Waaaaaaaaaaaaah!
All over an onion.

Wild Black Crows

Oh the wild black crows
The wild black crows
Fly far away to where nobody knows,
Where nobody knows and nobody goes,
Nobody knows
But the wild black crows.

Old Snake Has Gone To Sleep

Sun shining bright on the mountain rock
Old snake has gone to sleep.
Wild flowers blooming round the mountain rock
Old snake has gone to sleep.
Bees buzzing near the mountain rock
Old snake has gone to sleep.
Sun shining warm on the mountain rock
Old snake has gone to sleep.

Those Crazy Crows

Those crazy crows on ragged wing
Fly over the woods
They never sing
They screech and they scream
But they never sing
Those crazy crows
They never sing.

How Do You Know It's Spring?

How do you know it's Spring?
And how do you know it's Fall?
Suppose your eyes were always shut
And you couldn't see at all.
Could you smell and hear the Spring?
And could you feel the Fall?

Song Of Summer

Here comes a bunny
The first to stray
Out of April
And into May.

And here comes a robin
The first to fly
Out of June
And into July.

Here are the fireflies
Last to remember
The end of August
And first of September.

And here comes a caterpillar
The last to creep
Out of summer
And into sleep.

Fall Of The Year

The animals began to grow more fur,
The grey kitten sat by the fire to purr,
South flying birds passed overhead,
The leaves turned brown, the leaves turned red,
Then they tumbled down and blew away
Over the frosty ground all in one day.

Darkness came before the night,
The air grew cold enough to bite,
Chrysanthemums were shaggy yellow,
The pumpkin looked a fierce old fellow,
The world's on fire in the cold clear air
Autumn, autumn everywhere.

The Leaves Fall Down

One by one the leaves fall down
From the sky come falling one by one
And leaf by leaf the summer is done
One by one by one by one.

Cadence

There is music I have heard
Sharper than the song of bird
Sweeter still while still unheard
There beyond the inner ear.
Softer than the sounds I hear
Softer than the ocean's swell
In the caverns of a shell,
Tinier than cutting wings
Of flying birds and little things,
Like a cat's paw in the night
Or a rabbit's frozen fright.
This is the music I have heard
In the cadence of the word
Not spoken yet
And not yet heard.

About These Poems

Fourteen of the poems in this book are here printed for the first time. Eleven first appeared elsewhere as noted below. All are now the property of Margaret Wise Brown's sister, Roberta B. Rauch, and may not be reproduced without the written permission of the publisher.

"Four Fishing Boats" first appeared in *The Fish With The Deep Sea Smile*, E. P. Dutton & Co., 1938.

"Fish Song" first appeared in *The Fish With The Deep Sea Smile*.

"The Fish With The Deep Sea Smile" first appeared in *The Fish With The Deep Sea Smile*.

"Secret Song" first appeared in *Book Of Knowledge Annual*, 1952.

"The Bear And The Butterfly" first appeared in *Good Housekeeping*, June, 1949.

"Little Donkey Close Your Eyes" first appeared in *The Fish With The Deep Sea Smile*.

"How Do You Know It's Spring?" first appeared in *The Fish With The Deep Sea Smile*.

"The Sad Sliced Onion" first appeared in *Story Parade*, March, 1946.

"Wild Black Crows" first appeared in a slightly different version in *The Fish With The Deep Sea Smile*.

"Those Crazy Crows" first appeared in *The Fish With The Deep Sea Smile*.

"Fall Of The Year" first appeared in *The Fish With The Deep Sea Smile*.